second edition

Secret Boys' Business®

Written by

Rose Stewart
Fay Angelo
Heather Anderson

Illustrated by

Jeff Taylor

SGB Publishing Pty Ltd

CONTENTS

- **4** People grow and change all through their lives
- **8** About puberty
- **10** Some changes which happen during puberty
- **12** How babies are made
- **14** Signs that puberty has started
- **16** Hormones
- **18** Things are looking hairy!
- **19** Shaving
- **20** Volcanic eruptions – Pimples
- **22** Smelly bits
- **24** What a blast! – Voice changes
- **25** Changes down under
- **26** All about penises
- **28** Foreskins
- **29** Circumcision
- **30** Erections

32 All about testicles
35 Sperm facts
38 Sticky business – Wet dreams
40 Masturbation – Hands on info
42 Moody times
44 Coping with moods
46 Friends, girlfriends and boyfriends
48 Your body, your rights
50 Feeling good about your body
52 Tips for looking great
54 Final message
58 Hints for mums, dads, and other significant adults
64 Other books in this series

People grow and change

all through their lives

A boy's journey to manhood

Puberty is when your body gradually changes

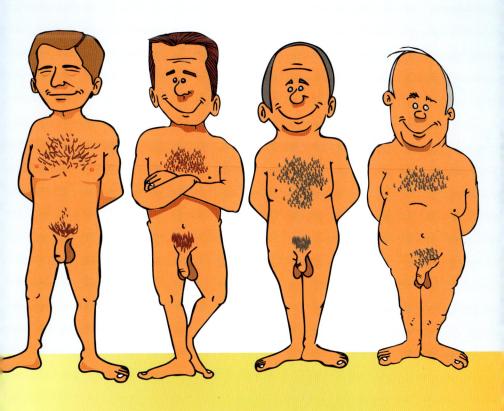

from the body of a boy to the body of a man.

Where are you on this journey?

About puberty

Puberty changes the way our bodies look and work, and the way we think and feel.

A boy gradually changes into a man

His body becomes bigger and stronger.

His brain develops so he is able to think about more difficult things.

Acceleration due to gravity = ?
Volume of a cone = ?
5 km = ? miles
$9 \times 4y = 7z$

His body changes so that he can become a father in the future if he chooses.

When will it happen?

When your body is the right size and shape for you it will begin to change.

Some boys begin puberty as young as 8.
While others may not start until 16.

It's OK if you change earlier or later.

Your body will do what is right for you.

Some changes which

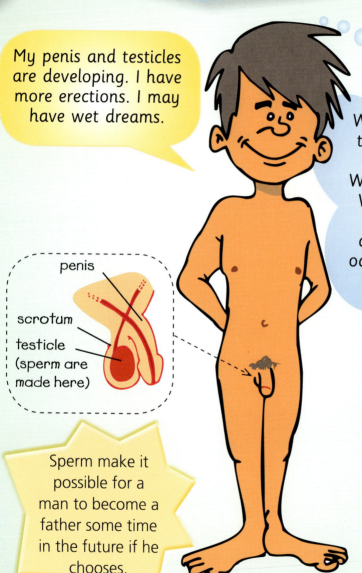

My penis and testicles are developing. I have more erections. I may have wet dreams.

We are growing taller, stronger and smarter. We are hungrier. We have body hair, pimples and BO (body odour). We have sexy feelings.

penis
scrotum
testicle (sperm are made here)

Sperm make it possible for a man to become a father some time in the future if he chooses.

happen during puberty

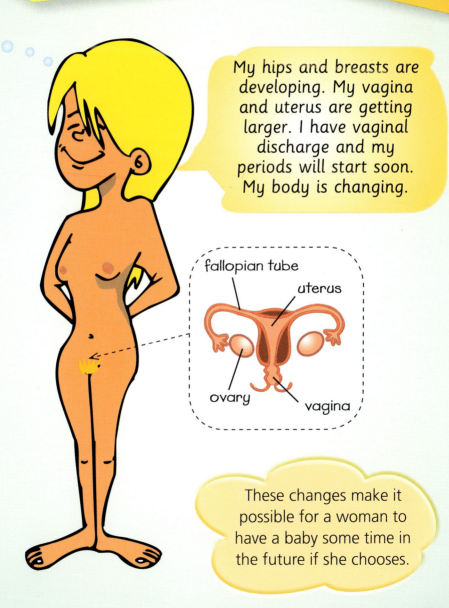

My hips and breasts are developing. My vagina and uterus are getting larger. I have vaginal discharge and my periods will start soon. My body is changing.

fallopian tube
uterus
ovary
vagina

These changes make it possible for a woman to have a baby some time in the future if she chooses.

How babies are made

A baby is made when sperm from a male joins with an egg from a female. This can happen as a result of sexual intercourse when a man's penis is in a woman's vagina.

Their bodies move together. This can feel good for both of them. After a short time semen containing sperm comes out of the man's penis and into the woman's vagina.

The sperm travels up through the woman's uterus and into her fallopian tubes. If one strong sperm joins with an egg, a baby begins to form.

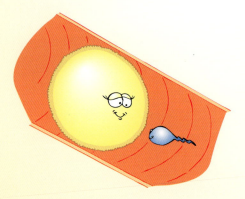

The egg is very small, about the size of a 'full stop'. Sperm are so small we can only see them with a microscope.

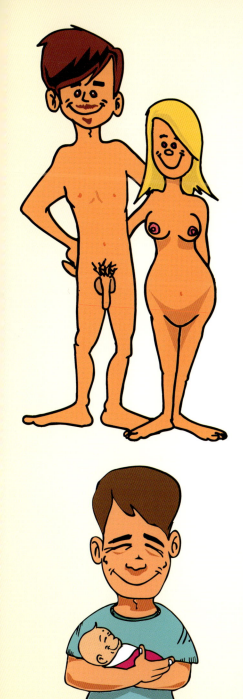

The developing baby moves down the woman's fallopian tube to her uterus.

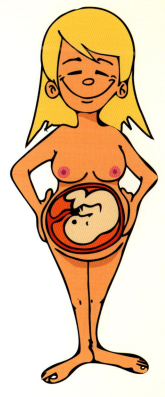

The uterus has a lining of blood and nutrients to feed the baby. The baby stays in the uterus, growing and developing for 9 months. Then it is ready to be born.

Signs that puberty

- Pubic hair
- Underarm hair
- Testicles produce more testosterone

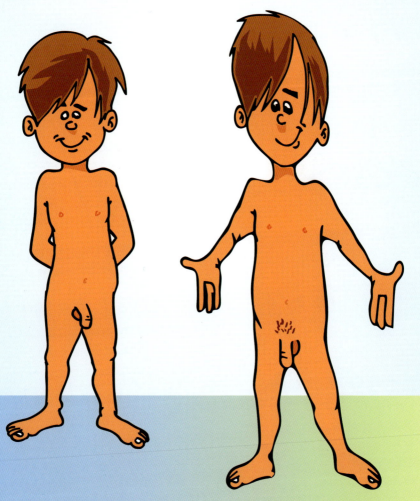

has started

- Growth spurt
- More erections
- Testicles begin sperm production

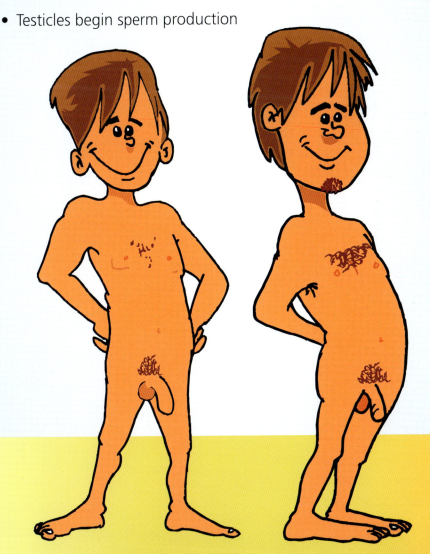

Hormones

At puberty a boy's body produces more male hormones. Hormones contain chemical messages. They travel in the blood causing the body to gradually change from a boy to a man.

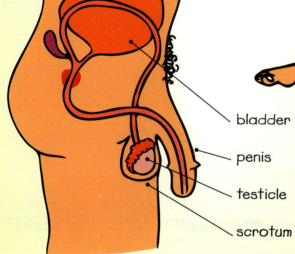

bladder

penis

testicle

scrotum

The most important male hormone is testosterone which is made in the testicles.

Every boy's body will change at different ages and in different ways.

Every boy will become bigger and stronger. Heights will vary greatly.

This is normal.

Things are **look**ing hairy!

Hair may grow in funny places,

Over shoulders, necks and faces,

Legs and thighs, and knees and toes.

Sometimes even up your nose!

On your arms across your back,

Sprouting out of various cracks.

Please don't think that you'll look bad ...

You'll end up handsome just like Dad!

When hair grows on your face you might need to start shaving.

Electric shavers and safety razors are easy to use.

Aftershave helps prevent shaving rash. Talk to your Dad or an older friend about cuts and rashes.

Volcanic eruptions – Pimples

At puberty, skin becomes more oily. Pimples form when oil glands become blocked.

Things which may help:

- Wash your face twice a day.
- Try not to touch pimples.

- Pimple cream from the chemist.
- Eat healthy food and drink lots of water.
- Exercise regularly.

If you are worried about pimples, ask the doctor for advice.

Smelly bits

Hormones make you sweat more and your body can smell.

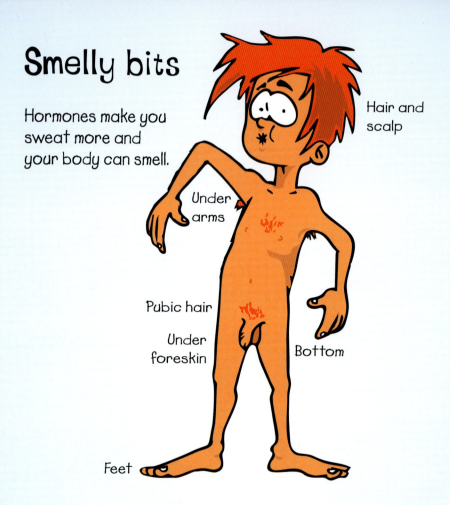

Hair and scalp
Under arms
Pubic hair
Under foreskin
Bottom
Feet

Phew! You could use some deodorant!

Handy hints

Shower daily.

Regularly shampoo your hair.

Use deodorant.

Put on clean underwear every day.

Change clothes and wear cotton socks for sport.

Wear a cotton T-shirt under your shirt to avoid sweat patches.

Air your sneakers. Wash the insole carefully, or change it.

What a blast! - Voice changes

At puberty your voice box gets bigger.

You can see your 'Adam's Apple'.

← Adam's apple

You may hear some surprising squeaks or crackles, highs or lows when you speak. People will say your voice is 'Breaking'.

Gradually your voice gets deeper.

Changes down under

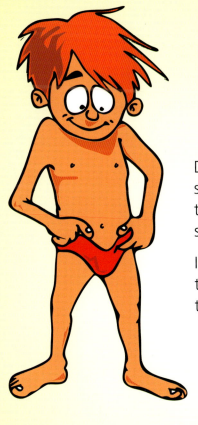

During puberty, the penis, scrotum and testicles will start to get bigger. The testicles will start to produce sperm.

It is the male hormone, testosterone, which makes this happen.

All about penises

Penises come in various sizes.
Different colours, shapes and guises.
Longer, thinner, short or thick,
Different names, Cock, Willie, Dick.
A curve to the left, a bend to the right,
Makes each one a different sight.
So if you wonder about your form,
Remember, to be different is the NORM!

Penises are for:

- Urinating
- Ejaculating sperm and semen
- Sexual pleasure

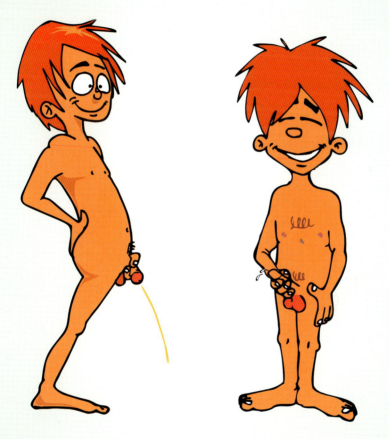

The penis has many nerve endings which make it sensitive.

The tip or head is the most sensitive part.

The long part of the penis is called the shaft.

Foreskins

Baby boys are born with a foreskin.

This is a fold of skin which covers the head of the penis.

Small glands under the foreskin produce smegma.

Smegma is a white creamy substance which helps the foreskin move easily over the head of the penis.

Boys with a foreskin need to wash it carefully when they are in the shower. Gently pull back the foreskin and wash away the smegma or it will smell.

Uncircumcised penis

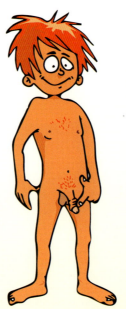
Uncircumcised penis – foreskin pulled back

Washing under the foreskin

Circumcision

Some boys have had their foreskin removed. This small operation is called 'circumcision'.

A small piece of skin is carefully removed by a doctor. After this operation the head of the penis is no longer covered by foreskin.

Circumcised penis

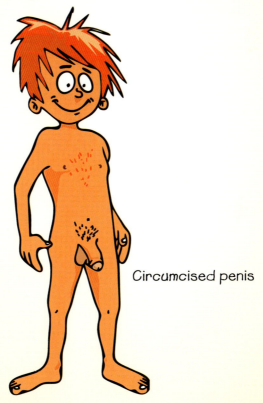

Circumcised penis

Penises perform exactly the same functions if they are circumcised or uncircumcised.

Erections

An erection happens when extra blood flows into the erectile tissue in the penis, making it bigger, straight and stiff.

All males have erections, even babies and little boys get them sometimes. This can feel nice.

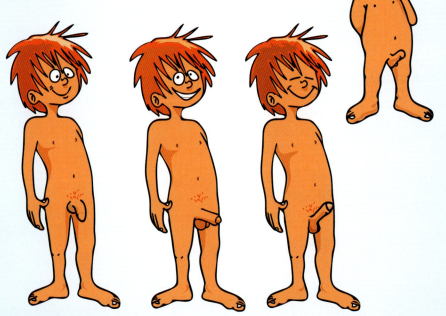

During puberty, erections happen more often.

> Clothing rubbing against your penis, touching yourself or sexy thoughts may cause an erection.

Some other names for an erection are a 'hard on', 'stiffie' or 'boner'.

Embarassing erections

During puberty, erections can happen when you are having sexy thoughts, or for no reason. This can be embarrassing.

Unwanted erections will go away more quickly if you concentrate on something else, e.g. say your 7 times tables backwards.

If you wear loose clothes, erections will be less noticeable.

All about testicles

Testicles slowly increase in size from birth to adulthood. Testicles are often called 'balls'.

Baby

Adult

Temperature control

The testicles hang in a bag of skin called the scrotum.

The scrotum helps to contol the temperature of the testicles. This is important for healthy sperm production.

When the body is hot, the scrotum stretches so the testicles hang further away from the body and become cooler. When it is cold the scrotum shrinks and moves the testicles closer to the body for extra warmth.

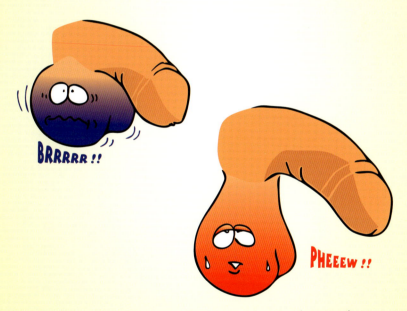

To be more comfortable, one testicle hangs lower than the other.

> Wear clothing that allows free movement of the testicles.

Taking care of your testicles

The testicles are very sensitive body parts and need protection during contact sport.

 Cricketers' box

A knock in the 'balls' is very painful. If the pain does not go away soon, you need to tell an adult you can trust.

Check your testicles regularly for lumps. You could do this in the shower. If you feel a lump, have it checked out by a doctor.

Sperm facts

The testicles produce more testosterone once puberty begins. Testosterone triggers the testicles to make sperm.

Up to one billion sperm are produced each day in the testicles.

Sperm make it possible for a male to become a father.

Sperm facts (cont.)

During puberty your body produces sperm and semen.

Millions of sperm are produced each day in the testicles. They continue to produce sperm for the rest of your life.

Sperm are so small they can only be seen through a microscope.

Semen is a whitish fluid which carries and nourishes the sperm. Sperm mixes with semen then comes out of the body through the erect penis. It comes out in little spurts, about a teaspoonful altogether. This is called ejaculation.

This gives you a very nice feeling called an orgasm.

A muscle near the bladder prevents urine coming out at the same time as semen.

Males have lots of erections but usually only ejaculate during:

- a wet dream
- masturbation
- sexual intercourse.

You don't ejaculate every time you have an erection

Sticky business - Wet dreams

Once sperm and semen are being made, some boys will have 'wet dreams'.

A wet dream is when a male ejaculates semen and sperm during his sleep.

Sometimes when a boy has a very sexy or exciting dream, his penis becomes erect and he ejaculates. This is normal.

He might wake with a very nice feeling. This is an orgasm.

Some boys will not wake up when they have a wet dream. The next morning they may notice some semen on their pyjamas. This washes out easily.

Some boys have wet dreams often, others once or twice, and some boys never have them.

Masturbation – Hands on info

Hormones are responsible for sexy thoughts and feelings.

You may have tingly enjoyable feelings in your body and penis. Some males choose to masturbate when they have sexy feelings.

This should be done in private.

Masturbation is rubbing the penis. It usually causes exciting, enjoyable feelings, leading to orgasm and ejaculation.

An orgasm is a really nice, strong, tingly feeling in this area that lasts for a short time. It leaves you feeling warm and relaxed.

Masturbation is normal.

Most boys masturbate – some often and some occasionally.

It's okay to masturbate in private.

Some masturbation myths

You will go blind.

Your penis will drop off.

You will run out of sperm.

These myths are not true

If you are worried about a masturbation myth, check it out with a trusted adult.

Moody times

At puberty, hormones not only change the way our bodies look and work, they also change the way we think and feel.

Your feelings may change quickly.

You might find yourself:
- Feeling misunderstood.
- Arguing with family, teachers or friends.
- Wanting to be by yourself.
- Feeling angry.
- Out of control.
- Sad or crying.
- Feeling lonely.

This is not much fun!

But also you might be:
- Having a fabulous time with friends.
- Thoughtful and supportive of others.
- Telling great jokes.

- Increasingly independent.
- More responsible.
- Trusted to make choices.

- Very energetic.

Talk about your feelings

It is normal to feel sad or angry at times, but if these feelings don't improve, you need to talk to your family, your teacher, a counsellor or a doctor.

Coping with moods

Things which might help

If you are feeling grumpy, angry or fed up, these things might help:

Burn off some energy
- Shoot some hoops
- Walk the dog
- Ride your bike
- Pound the punching bag
- Beat the drums

Give yourself some time out

- Listen to some music
- Play an electronic game
- Spend some time in your room

- Strum a guitar
- Watch TV
- Spend some time with your family or friends

Think more helpful thoughts

- Change from negative thinking to positive thinking.

Everyone is making me angry.

I am angry but I can do lots of things to calm down.

- Plan to do something you really enjoy.

Friends, girlfriends, boyfriends

At puberty it is normal for boys to become more aware of girls and to think a lot about having a girlfriend.

Some boys get red in the face when they are around girls. They feel hot and sweaty and awkward. This can be embarrassing.

Thinking about love and sex is something that happens a lot from puberty onwards.

Many boys find that during puberty they think about one particular person in this way. This is called a crush.

You might have a crush on someone with whom you would not expect to have a romantic relationship.

If a boy has a crush on another boy or man this does not necessarily mean that he is gay.

However a few boys are naturally same-sex-attracted. This can be a confusing and worrying time for a while.

Your body, your rights

> We are the boss of our bodies.
> Our bodies are private.

We have the right to decide who can see or touch our bodies.

There are very few times when another person will need to look at or touch your private parts. One example would be if you need a medical check.

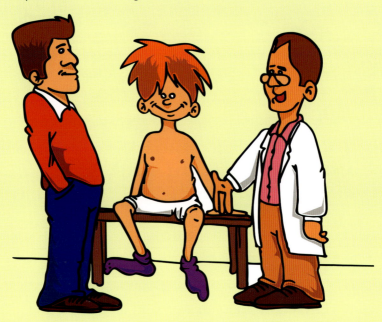

Feeling good about your body

Lots of boys worry about how they look. This is normal but not helpful.

Bodies come in many different shapes and sizes and change at different ages.

Body shape and size are influenced by our 'genes' which come to us in our father's sperm and mother's egg. These genes are mixed up to give each baby a new, unique combination.

Many boys worry about their physique or body shape. There is a wide range of healthy physiques, depending on age, height and body type.

> You can check with your doctor to see what is OK for you.

By eating healthy food, having enough sleep and taking regular exercise, our bodies will be the best they can be.

> Remember, whatever your physique, you can be fit, healthy and happy, and have great friends!

Tips for looking great

Posture

Stand straight and tall. Stomach in, shoulders back and head up.

Clothes

Choose clothes that you feel good in. Put them in the wash regularly to keep them clean and fresh.

Hair

Clean, well-kept hair always looks good. Experiment with different haircuts, styles, and products to achieve the look you want.

Nails

Keep your nails clean and well shaped. A nail clipper is easy to use with either hand.

Teeth

Brush twice a day. Ask your dentist about the best way to floss.

Looking your best will make you feel good about yourself.

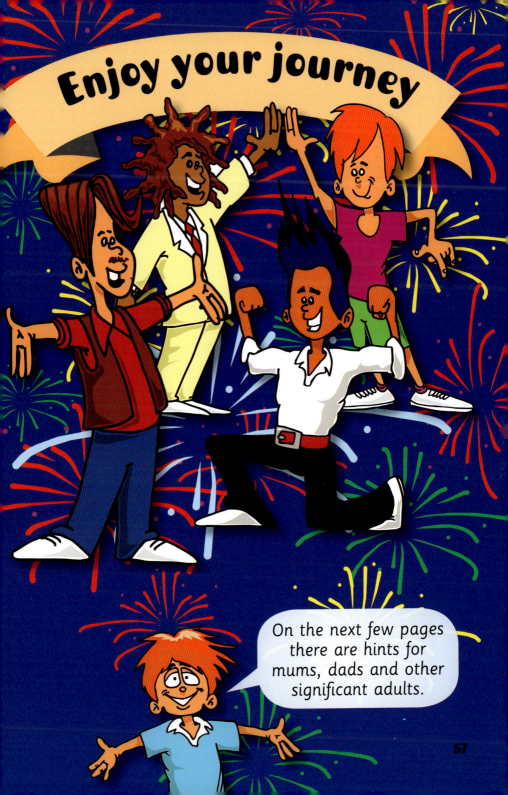

Hints for mums, dads, and

Forward planning

- Read *Secret Boys Business*® a few times, becoming comfortable with the vocabulary and subject matter.
- Think carefully about how you will use the book, and how you will present it to your son. Which topics will you follow-up with him?
- Your reaction to your son's changes will have a lasting impression on his confidence and self esteem.
- A positive attitude towards growth and change will empower boys to become confident young men.

When to talk about puberty changes

- Parents can talk about differences between boys and girls, how babies are made, and body changes from the time children are very young. Don't wait until puberty to talk about these things.
- Discussion about puberty needs to be part of everyday communication and not a 'one off chat'.
- When puberty is imminent, more specific discussion can take place about body changes.
- Keep the lines of communication open and be prepared to discuss any queries or comments in a thoughtful way.
- If questions are asked at awkward moments, say that you will talk about it later in private. Be certain to follow up as soon as possible.

other significant adults

Vocabulary

- Families often develop their own language for private body parts and their functions. It is important for boys to know correct names and appropriate language for different situations, such as talking to the doctor.

- Encourage your son to become confident in communicating with the doctor. When he is a little older, he will be able to make appointments independently to talk about private matters.

- It is good for boys to understand the changes girls experience at puberty and to have appropriate vocabulary. See *More Secret Girls Business*®, also in this series.

Healthy bodies, healthy self-esteem

- Puberty changes can have a negative impact on self esteem.
- It is important to assist boys to develop self-confidence and feelings of self-worth.
- Boys who begin puberty earlier than their peers may feel embarrassed about their size, body development and voice changes.
- Boys who are smaller, less physically developed and who experience puberty later, may sometimes develop low self-esteem.
- Parents need to be aware of different expectations depending on height.
  - Tall boys are often expected to be more mature and accept added responsibility. Because of their size, their behaviour may be perceived as challenging, bullying or rude.
  - Boys who are small are often treated as if they are younger than their age, overlooked for tasks, and passed over for leadership roles and responsibilities.
- Encourage all members of the family to be respectful about puberty changes and not to embarrass, joke or tease.
- Like young women, young men take on board messages they see and hear about weight and body shape. If your son is present, avoid discussing personal weight issues or being critical of your own body shape.
- Be aware of messages about body image in the media and discuss these with your son.
- Value your son's positive qualities, and take care to avoid negative comments about his body shape.
- Model healthy living, eating and exercising.
- Ensure there is a range of nutritious foods available for snacks and prepare healthy meals.
- Encourage water instead of sugary drinks.

- Exercise should be a regular part of the daily routine.
- Establish a regular sleep routine ensuring adequate sleep each night.
- To ensure good quality sleep, electronic devices should not be used or monitored during sleep times.

Feelings

- Listen carefully to your son when he is talking about his worries. Acknowledge and validate his feelings.
- Don't feel that you have to take responsibility for solving his problems. It is more helpful to coach him to problem-solve, discussing possible courses of action and their outcomes.
- Boys should know it is OK to show their emotions.
- During puberty it is even more important for boys to have positive male role models.
- All boys undergoing changes at puberty will have self-conscious moments.
- Be aware that boys may be emotional, short tempered, over sensitive and angry at times. Avoid confrontation as you may exacerbate the situation. Deal with it later when things are calmer.
- All problem behaviours need to be dealt with and boys taught to be respectful to family and friends.

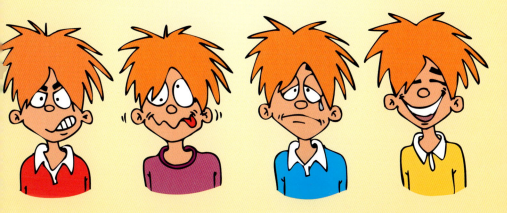

Friends, boyfriends and girlfriends

- It is normal to have friends who are boys and friends who are girls. Reinforce with boys that this is normal and different from a romantic relationship.
- Taunts about girlfriend/boyfriend relationships make many boys uncomfortable and can be a form of bullying. If this becomes a problem, discuss it with his teacher.
- Teasing and bullying that names someone as 'gay' is not uncommon amongst peers when there is conflict. All adults should deal with this in a firm but positive manner so that name calling is clearly not acceptable.
- *The Secret Business of Relationships, Love and Sex*™ book has fantastic information about teenage relationships.

Same sex attraction

- Some boys wonder or worry if they are 'same-sex attracted'. It is important that adults do not give negative messages about sexual orientation.
- If you need advice about same sex attraction or have any queries about your son's sexuality, contact your general practitioner or local family planning association.

Privacy – a very important issue

- At puberty there is a need for more privacy in the home. Family members should knock and wait for acknowledgement before entering bathrooms or bedrooms which are occupied.

- Parents' reaction to masturbation can have lasting effects on a boy's self-esteem and sexuality. Negative reactions are not helpful. Respect his privacy!

Protective behaviours – personal safety

- Discuss appropriate sexual behavior, what is OK and what is not.

- Be aware that boys can be sexually abused.

- Boys need to know what to do and who to tell if they experience inappropriate sexual behavior.

- If your son tells you about sexual abuse, remain calm, believe him, and never blame. Protect him from further abuse.

- Any concerns can be discussed with your local CASA (Centre Against Sexual Assault).

- There is a lot of inappropriate sexual information on the internet. Discuss this with boys and monitor internet use.

Books written and published by
Secret Girls' Business®

Please visit us at www.secretgb.com or email at secretgb@hotmail.com